NARROW GAUGE STEAM
OUT OF PORTMADOC

twenty-five years of the Festiniog Railway

NORMAN F. GURLEY

BRADFORD BARTON

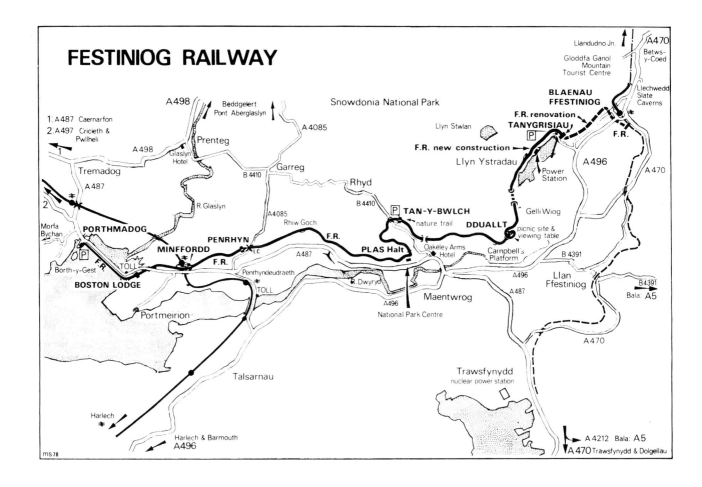

FESTINIOG RAILWAY

Frontispiece: Afon Dwyryd and the Vale of Ffestiniog make an attractive backcloth as 'Mountaineer' heads a light train down through Coed Dduallt. Of legal necessity the Festiniog Railway retains the English version of its name for all official purposes, but adopts a bilingual attitude where practicable.   (N. Gurley)

© copyright D. Bradford Barton Ltd 1980   ISBN 0 85153 380 9

printed and bound by CTP Ltd for Top Link Ltd

for the publishers

D. BRADFORD BARTON LTD · TRURO · CORNWALL · ENGLAND

INTRODUCTION

In June 1954, after spadework by many people over the three preceding years, Alan Pegler and his nominees took over control of the Festiniog Railway Company. More than a year was to follow before the first revenue-earning passenger train of the new era trundled out of Portmadoc and across the Cob to Boston Lodge and back, but that was a year packed with activity by a rapidly growing band of voluntary workers. Many of these were present when the 'new' administration celebrated its Silver Jubilee in June 1979.

This book is a pictorial record of those intervening twenty five years. It does not claim to be a pictorial history - that would imply a commitment to ilustrate every milestone and every development within a great many facets of railway operation, some of which are by no means photogenic. Indeed, a few notable events of the period do not seem to have been photographed; no pictures have come to light of the chain shunt enacted at Boston Lodge in the summer of 1955 to enable first the Simplex and then 'Prince' to run round the two coach train of that historic season. I remember watching the operation during my first working visit over August Bank Holiday; I do not recall, unfortunately, even considering taking a photograph...

For a pictorial history, there may probably be too many views of trains - albeit in the charge of fourteen different locomotives, for which I make no apology. Offices and permanent way depots, machine shops and builders' yards are all part and parcel of a busy railway; less so of a successful photographic album. I have tried not to neglect some human interest; personalities have always featured prominently in the story of the Festiniog Railway, sometimes harmonising, sometimes clashing, but invariably adding spice to the saga of metal and money, slate and tourism, coal and oil.

The Festiniog is not, in fact, an easy railway to photograph. The inaccessibility of many long stretches, as well as the tight clearances throughout, limit the casual photographer to stations and a few well-known locations. My employment on the line for sixteen years, latterly as Permanent Way Ganger, gave me an advantage in this regard, as has since 1972 the title of Official Photographer, although photography has always been and remains strictly a hobby. It is not surprising that many of the contributors to these pages took their photographs while working at the lineside. I thank them all, not forgetting those whose offerings eventually had to be turned down, very often for reasons which had nothing to do with quality, and those who searched diligently but unsuccessfully for mislaid negatives. I am grateful to Allan Garraway, Arthur Lambert and Russel Burridge for their constructive comments. The choice of photographs, however - from more than three thousand at my disposal - is my own. Many were selected simply because I found them pleasing; I hope the reader will share some of that pleasure.

FFESTINIOG, GWYNEDD   NORMAN F. GURLEY

In 1954 the intrepid explorer following the largely derelict route of the Festiniog Railway would be finding the going slightly easier afte this cutting seven miles from Portmadoc. Above 400' the impediments progress on foot tended to take the form of flooded cuttings and improvised livestock fencing rather than impenetrable growth.

(Geoff Charl

At Harbour Station, Portmadoc, Manager Robert Evans maintained a vigil throughout the nine years of closure, while efforts both to resurrect and to abandon the line met with an equal lack of success. Eventually, a year after Alan Pegler had gained control and with reopening well in prospect, Mr Evans retired from the scene, but his earlier presence had ensured the preservation of a wealth of material for the railway's archives.

(Geoff Charles)

At Boston Lodge workshops and sheds, nearly a mile from Portmadoc over the embankment known as the Cob, another elderly gentleman, the Reverend Timmy Phillips, fought a good fight with weapons of corrugated iron and rotting timber to keep scrap merchants and souvenir hunters at bay. Paths were worn by visitors seeking weaknesses in Timmy's defences.
(Geoff Charles)

Although a scheme to start restoration from the Blaenau Ffestiniog end was examined, it was almost inevitable that early activity was centred around Portmadoc and Boston Lodge. In the middle of the line, Tan-y-Bwlch slumbered peacefully, disturbed only by the comings and goings of the residents, erstwhile lady-stationmaster Bessie Jones and her husband Will.
(D. Rendell)

Will Jones had been employed on the track for 24 years before closure in 1946, and not long thereafter he was back at work, imparting his rather specialised knowledge of maintaining chaired narrow-gauge track to enthusiastic but very green volunteers.
(P.Q. Treloar)

The first active
locomotive of the new
era was a Simplex
petrol tractor,
appropriately built
for battlefield
service in the First
World War, later to
be named 'Mary Ann'.
This excursion up the
partially cleared
line on 30 May 1955
ended in mishap, as
they often did, on
this occasion a few
hundred yards from
Tan-y-Bwlch.
   (Hugh Ballantyne)

FESTINIOG RAILWAY LOCOMOTIVES 1954-1979 (Apart from building details, information given relates to the 1954-1979 period only)

Locomotive	Building Details	Acquired	Overhauls Completed	Aprx.FR Mileage	Notes
'Prince' 0-4-0STT	George England 1863		1955/62/	40,000	Out of use since 1968. Rebuilt and oil-firing conversion nearing completion 1979
'Princess' 0-4-0STT	George England 1863				Displayed at Portmadoc 1963-69; Blaenau Ffestiniog from 1969
'Palmerston' 0-4-0STT	George England 1864				Sold to Group Five Engine Assoc. in 1974 for restoration
'Welsh Pony' 0-4-0STT	George England 1867				Awaiting repair
'Merddin Emrys' 0-4-4-0T(F)	Boston Lodge 1879		1961/79	60,000	Oil-fired from 1973
'Taliesin' 0-4-4-0T(F)	Boston Lodge 1886				Body stored for preservation from 1972, reverting to original name 'Livingstone Thompson'
'Earl of Merioneth' 0-4-4-0T(F)	Boston Lodge 1979			1,500	New, oil-fired, loco using parts from old bogies
'Volunteer' 0-6-0ST	Pecket (2050), 1944	1957			ex-N.E. Gas Board, Harrogate; awaiting repair
'Linda' 0-4-0St	Hunslet (590), 1893	1962	1970	107,000	ex-Penrhyn Quarry Railway (on loan until end 1963)0-4-0STT(1962)2-4-0STT(1970)
'Blanche' 0-4-0STT	Hunslet (589), 1893	1963	1972	115,000	ex-Penrhyn Quarry Railway (0-4-0ST): 2-4-0STT(1972) Oil-fired from 1971
'K1' 0-4-0+0-4-0	Garratt Beyer, Peacock (5792) 1909	1966			To N.R.M. York on loan 1976
'Mountaineer' 2-6-2T	Alco (57156) 1916	1967		60,000	ex-T.P.T.(France) via J. Ransom. Nameplates fitted 1969 Oil-fired from 1971
'Moel Tryfan' 0-6-4T(F)	Vulcan (738) 1875				ex-Welsh Highland Rly: Scrapped 1954
'Britomart' 0-4-0ST	Hunslet (707) 1899				ex-Pen-yr-Orsedd Quarry 1965: Privately owned by group of staff (originally) and volunteers
'Kidbrooke' 0-4-0ST	W. Barclay (2043) 1917				Stored on Festiniog Railway 1961-70 Privately owned by R. Hilton
'Bimmelbahn' 0-8-0	O.& K. 1934				ex-DR 99 3462. Stored on F.R. 1972-78 Privately owned by J. Snell and associates
'Mary Ann' 4wPM(and TVO)	Motor Rail (596?) 1917	1961		16,500	4wDM (·1961) Simplex Nameplates fitted 1971
'Moelwyn' 0-4-0PM	Baldwin (49604) 1918		1956/67	60,000	0-4-0DM (1956) 2-4-0DM (1957) Nameplates fitted 1956
'Busta' 2-2-0PM	W.H.R. (Austin engine)	1955			Dismantled 1965
'Upnor Castle' 4wDM Planet	Hibberd (3687) 1954	1968	1971	25,000	ex-Lodge Hill & Upnor Railway, Kent, via Welshpool & Llanfair Lt. Railway
'Moel Hebog' 0-4-0DM 'Mines'	Hunslet (4113) 1955	1969	1975	7,000	ex-Shaw Cross Colliery, Yorkshire Nameplates fitted 1975
'Tyke' 4wDH	Hunslet (2290) 1941	1962	1962		Dismantled
'Alistair' 4wDM	Ruston (201970) 1940	1968		6,000	ex-H.A. Bierrum. Under repair 1979
'Jane' 4wDM Simplex	Motor Rail (8565) 1940	1971		15,000	ex-St. Albans Sand & Gravel via Col. A. Campbell, Dduallt. Name carried 1972-76
'Diana' 4wDM Simplex	Motor Rail (21579) 1957	1974	1974	7,000	ex-Minworth Sewage Works. Name carried 1974-76
'Andrew' 4wDM	Ruston (193984) 1939	1974			ex-Smith & Son (Raunds). Dismantled for repair 1979
'Monster' 4wDM	Boston Lodge	1974			To R. Morris 1976
'Sludge' 4wDM	Lister (41545) 1954	1976	1976		ex-Finham Sewage Works via Stoneleigh
'Sandra' 4wDM Simplex	Motor Rail (22119) 1956	1977		3,000	ex-Anglia Water Authority
'The Grogan' 4wBEV	Wingrove & Rogers (5537) 1956	1975			ex-Wheal Jane, Cornwall. Used during tunnel boring. Sold 1979
- 4wDM Simplex	Motor Rail (8788?) 1943?				Owned by Col.A. Campbell; ex-St. Albans Sand & Gravel, 1966
- 2-2-0PM	Wickham	c1960		10,000	Motorised PW trolley; ex-BR.
'Stefcomatic' 2-2-0DH	Matisa (48589) 1955	1968	1977		Ballast Tamper, ex-BR(S).
- 4wDM Simplex	Motor Rail (8788?) 1943?				Owned by Col.A. Campbell; ex-St.Albans Sand & Gravel, 1966

('4w' denotes driving wheels coupled by chains or shafts, rather than by outside rods. Several of the smaller diesels were acquired, overhauled and donated by Area Groups of the Festiniog Railway Society)

For thirteen months after the take-over a major source of revenue was from sales of scrap metal, at a little under £3 per ton. A passenger service started between Portmadoc and Boston Lodge on 23 July 1955 with the Simplex hauling two coaches. 'Prince' was able to take over the duties within a fortnight, and handled nearly all the trains for the rest of the summer and throughout 1956. Although 'Prince' carried the number 2 for a while, Festiniog Railway locomotives are always referred to by name or occasionally by maker - for example Simplex, Planet, Alcor.

(P.B. Whitehouse)

With trains operatir
to Minffordd in 195€
Boston Lodge became
an intermediate halt
The turntables here
and at Blaenau
Ffestiniog had long
since fallen into
disuse, and with the
location of the uppe
terminus changing
regularly no seriou:
thought has been giv
to the turning of
tender locomotives f
the down journey.
(P.Q. Treloa

'Prince' stands at
Minffordd in May 19!
with an obviously
badly needed weed-
killing train, Thi:
wagon was previousl:
used to convey sea
water to Plas Tan-y-
Bwlch so that membe
of the Oakeley famil
and their guests cou
take brine baths.
The slate-slab
reception tank can
still be seen alongs
the track on the
hillside above the
Plas. (John Ranso

Anyone remembering a pre-1939 journey on the Festiniog Railway will have vivid recollections of the old Moelwyn tunnel - 730 suffocating yards long at a gradient of 1 in 116, steep enough to make the locomotives work hard and sometimes slip to a standstill on the wet rail. Travelling in the front coach of an up train with the window open was considered a certain cure for whooping-cough by local people. The motive power in this photograph is 'Busta' (see page 25).

(Ken Cribb)

One portion of the Festiniog Railway did not close in 1946 as part of the line formed a vital link between various slate quarries and the two standard-gauge goods yards, both of which had dual-gauge slate transshipment facilities. Here a quarry-owned diesel is propelling loaded slate wagons into the Western Region yard on 21 June 1956 over 1'11½" gauge track laid in 95 lb/yard bull-head rail.

(Brian Hilton)

soon as the
ndition of the track
uld permit, trains
re run through to
aenau to retrieve
gons and other items
value before
oposed road and hydro-
ectric works truncated
e Festiniog Railway
ove the Moelwyn tunnel.
could not have been
visaged at the time
at legal proceedings
secure a reasonable
asure of compensation
r this severance
uld drag on for
fteen years.
(Geoff Charles)

ime was short. On
1 June 1956 it can be
een the line had been
ut immediately beyond
North Western' - the
xchange station with
hat had been the L.M.S.
hen Festiniog trains
ast used it - for
onstruction of the
ccess road to
anygrisiau power
tation. Contractors
re dismantling the
tation canopy, which
as sold to raise
ssential funds and
till serves a useful
unction on winter
aturdays, protecting
pectators at Cae Clyd
ootball ground from
laenau's notoriously
eavy rainfall -
otalling on average
20 inches a year....
(Brian Hilton)

After much painstaking work behind the scenes - only those who helped to turn the handle when the cylinders were being re-bored by hand will know just how painstaking it was - double Fairlie 'Taliesin' ran trials at the end of 1956, and was turned out in grey primer for the Festiniog Railway Society's Annual General Meeting on 30 March 1957.

(N. Gurley)

Built at Boston Lodge in 1885, but not actually entering service until 1886, this locomotive was originally named 'Livingstone Thompson' - after a director of the Railway Company from 1836 to 1873 - and was renamed 'Taliesin' about 1931 following the withdrawal of the single Fairlie of that name. A further name change was made on 22 April 1961, when the Duke of Edinburgh's title 'Earl of Merioneth' was bestowed to the fireman's side and the Welsh version, ' Iarll Meirionnydd', to the driver's side.   (N. Gurley)

Tracks connecting t
Croesor Tramway,
later the Welsh
Highland Railway,
with the slate
wharves and Harbour
Station at Portmado
proved useful in 19
-55, when the Simpl
was able to park
quite close to a
filling station for
petrol. When this
facility was no
longer required, th
rails were
laboriously lifted
for re-use on the C
The work provided
particularly useful
experience for the
young volunteer on
the left, Alan Keef
who was later to
build up a thriving
light railway
contracting busines
Below: 'Prince'
mingles with the
traffic on Britanni
bridge in Portmadoc
after leaving rail
bolsters for loadin
in Madoc Street.
Road improvements
obliterated the
remaining track soo
afterwards.
(N. Gurle

When outshopped in 1956 with a Gardner diesel engine and, soon afterwards, with a pony truck, American-built 'Moelwyn' proved a more versatile machine than the Simplex and has since run a prodigious mileage, primarily on permanent way trains. No. 1 van's wooden frame did not stand the test of time so well and its body was relegated to lineside duties by the mid-1960s.   (John Alexander)

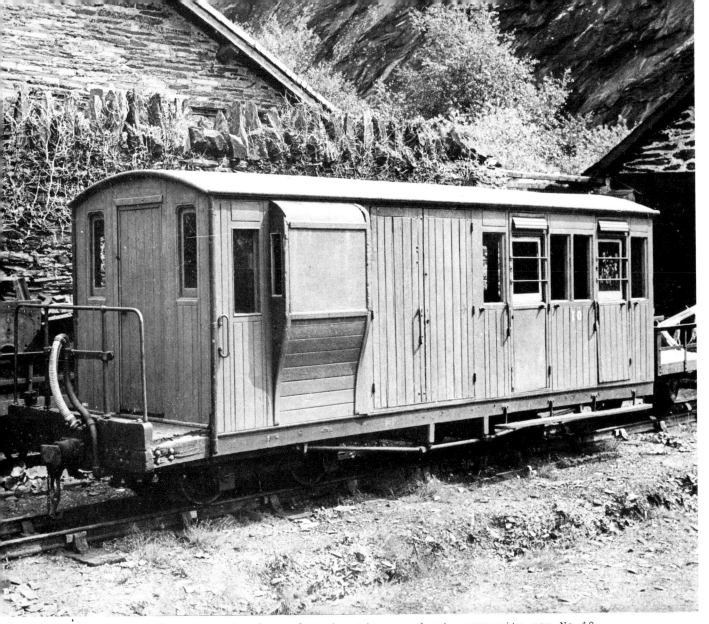

Another casualty of wooden frame deterioration was bogie composite van No.10.
Lacking the Simplex's armour plating, its guard's lookouts and glass-less windows
show indications of the battering received during early forays up the line.
Withdrawn from use in 1958, No.10 still awaits rebuilding, possibly as a
breakdown van or mobile messroom; some of the Society's Area Groups have been
tempted to tackle it as a homework project, but it is a little too large to be
accommodated in the average domestic garage!

(N. Gurley)

'Taliesin' taking the crossover into Minffordd loop with a train of coal empties from Boston Lodge to Minffordd yard. In the train is the Cleminson patent six-wheeled mineral wagon, the only survivor of a series of experimental vehicles built in the 1870s.
(John Alexander)

A tranquil scene in the sun at Boston Lodge, as the bottom bogie of brake-compo-buffet No.12 receives attention. To the right, in front of the Cleminson six-wheeler, is 'Busta', said to be an ex-Welsh Highland Railway permanent way trolley, which saw spasmodic service between January 1955 and the early 1960s. This was mainly on hilarious high-speed journeys between the works and Portmadoc hostelries, if Festiniog folklore is to be believed!
(Hugh Ballantyne)

1958 brought a major change, with trains running through to Tan-y-Bwlch from the start of the season without any fuss or preamble. The fuss, in fact, came in the following three years when the extra four miles of track deteriorated rapidly and the need to consolidate before advancing further was recognised. Tan-y-Bwlch was to remain the upper terminus for ten years. With only 'Taliesin' and 'Prince' to handle all traffic until 1961, the fifteen-mile round trip was quite long enough from the railway's point of view.

(John Ransom)

More passengers travelling twice as far created a rolling stock crisis during August 1958, something which has been experienced to a varying degree in the peak period of every year since. The 1958 remedy was for six men to work day and night to prepare a relief train of four-wheeled coaches, known individually as 'Bug boxes' and collectively as the 'Flying Flea'

(Ron Jarvis)

The green-and-ivory combination adopted in 1955 was sometimes known as the 'Woolworth's livery'. Whether or not this was meant to be complimentary, it is a fact that the cost, in terms of man hours in both application and maintenance, led to its downfall. Freshly applied to 'bow-sider' No.17 of 1876 it had an aesthetic appeal in 1959 that nothing on the Festiniog Railway of 1979 can match.

(Ron Jarvis)

Overhaul of double Fairlie 'Merddin Emrys' commenced at the end of 1958 and was to take two years. This impressive rivetted wagon-top boiler had been supplied by Vulcan Foundry in 1920, and after skilful repairs was to give a few more years service before being scrapped around 1970.   (Ron Jarvis)

During 1959 and 1960, the roads between Portmadoc harbour and Trawsfynydd were greatly improved in connection with the transporting of components for Trawsfynydd Atomic Power Station. A temporary level crossing took the main road across the railway while Rhiw Plas bridge, between Boston Lodge and Minffordd, was being rebuilt. The crossing keepers were kept busy over Whitsun 1960.
(N. Gurley)

The Festiniog Railway took away trains of rubble from the bridge works to reinforce culvert repairs further up the line, using anything with a floor and four wheels to clear the job.
(John Ransom)

By the end of 1960 'Prince' was in rather a sorry state below the waist and an offer of new cylinders free of charge was gratefully accepted. While awaiting delivery, the boiler and chassis presented a rather pathetic spectacle.

(John Alexander)

With 'Merddin Emrys' entering service on A.G.M. day 1961, the railway had two legendary Bards at its disposal for a few hours before the renaming of 'Taliesin', but it continued to enjoy the services of two double Fairlies for the rest of the year - and part of the next.

(Alastair Stirling)

A game of cat's cradle for Signals and Telegraphs Department volunteers, with a serious motive - eliminating the vulnerable pole route across the Cob by sharing a duct alongside the track with the Post Office. This duct, incidentally, has been a continual headache to the Permanent Way Department ever since!
(Dan Wilson)

1962 was a momento year for the Festiniog Railway it got off to a picturesque start New Year's Day, wh volunteers from Cambridge Universi took several hours to get their works train up the line Dduallt. Object o the exercise was t lifting of track components from th abandoned Moelwyn tunnel.
(Allan Garraw

Volunteering can be fun, but it takes a sense of humour to enjoy pushing four tons of notoriously stiff wagon up a 1 in 30 gradient on a curve with flangeways cut into turf....
(G. Adams)

nding locomotive problems were felt as early as Easter 1962. With 'Prince'
r repairs and 'Earl of Merioneth' being retubed, 'Merddin Emrys' developed
fective plug and, with a little assistance from 'Moelwyn' took nine coaches
a bogie wagon to Tan-y-Bwlch with only one regulator open.   Since 1962,
restation has deprived the 60' dry stone Cei Mawr - seen here - of much of
grandeur.
                                                              (John Alexander)

'Merddin's' firebox deteriorated and the Fairlie had to be taken out of service
early in July 1962. The Festiniog turned in desperation to the Penrhyn Quarry
Railway for assistance, and on 14 July 'Linda' arrived at Minffordd, looking
just a little like something by Patrick Stirling on the BR Lowmac on which she
was conveyed.
                                                              (John Alexander)

Within a few hours of arriving at Boston Lodge, 'Linda' took a trial train to
Cei Mawr and, soon afterwards, handled the Minffordd coal shunt with consummate
ease, her Penrhyn sand bucket being an unnecessary ornament. There were, of
course, several modifications to be made and vacuum brake to be fitted before
solo passenger work could be undertaken.
(N. Gurley)

On 25 July a loose rock dislodged itself from a garden wall at Penrhyn and derailed
very last bogie of the 10.30 train, breaking three axle-boxes. The train continued
without its observation car, and on its return the passengers were exchanged with
from the next train, walking happily past the obstruction. Through running was res
at mid-day, and after the customary overnight session at Boston Lodge the observati
car returned to service next morning.
(Alastair Sti

The trials and tribulations of 1962 were far from over, 'Prince' had returned to service, but frequently retired to Boston Lodge for attention. A broken piston head was eventually diagnosed and a temporary repair effected in yet another overnight stint.

(N. Gurley)

Without even the acquisition of a tender, 'Linda' coasts down towards Penrhyn from Tan-y-Bwlch on one of her first trial runs on the Festiniog. Although her potential was obvious, there were plenty of teething troubles, and nobody could have guessed that within seventeen years, she and sister 'Blanche' would have run over 100,000 miles each in Festiniog Railway service.   (Peter Barnfield)

'Taliesin' simmering
at Tan-y-Bwlch on a
summer day in 1960.
Although badly in
need of overhaul this
Fairlie, renamed
'Earl of Merioneth',
was the mainstay of
the service
throughout the
troubles of 1962.
(Ron Jarvis)

In 1963 'Prince' became a centenarian, and the event was not allowed to slip by
unnoticed. The extra publicity generated useful additional traffic, and
'Merddin Emrys' sometimes needed assistance with the heavy 14.20 train. Fresh
from overhaul, with improvements to framing (compare with page 13) and a Kylchap
cowl to boost the blast, 'Prince' was in excellent condition.   (N. Gurley)

'...rl of Merioneth'
...ft) entered shops
... an overhaul that
... to take four
...rs. With two of
...rything to be
...aired or replaced,
...rlie overhauls
...ariably take a
...g time, and
...gress is
...ticularly slow
...ing the summer
...ths when driving
...ters and minor
...s to stock in
...vice may leave no
...lled or semi-
...lled labour for
...g term projects.
          (N. Gurley)

An interesting innovation for the 1963 peak season was the working of the 15.00 train non-stop to Tan-y-Bwlch, provided the 14.20 cleared the section in time. The loadings eventually got a little too heavy for 'Prince' and 'Linda' - still officially only on loan from the Penrhyn Quarry Railway - took over the duty.

(Alastair Stirling)

The serpentine curves of Tan-y-Bwlch station held no artistic appeal for operating staff handling the two terminating trains together. Only after the main train had safely departed, with all doors secured and no small boys clinging to the coach balconies, could they relax and discuss the inadequacies of the layout and ill-defined platforms....   (N. Gurley)

1963 was a comparatively uneventful year from the operating point of view, apart from a period at the end of the season when a steam failure left diesel power on the 15.00. A protracted wait at Penhryn to pass the down train rather spoilt the crack express image.

(N. Gurley)

At the end of 1963 'Linda' was purchased from Penrhyn Quarry together with sister locomotive 'Blanche' and several miles of track. 'Blanche' was re-gauged and equipped with vacuum brake and tender before running trials, and is seen here in passenger service during 1964, still in Penrhyn Quarry livery.

(C.J. Stratmann)

Another 1963 acquisition, via the Society's White Rose Group, was Hudson Hunslet 'Tyke'. Unfortunately 'Tyke' proved very troublesome to start, and failed to make much of an impact.

(John Alexander)

The mid-1960s brought a revolution in the Festiniog Railway's permanent way techniques. Arrival at Minffordd in 1963 of double-head materials from the portion of line at Tanygrisiau acquired by the Electricity Board and in 1965 of bull-head track from the Penrhyn Railway, permitted full scale renewals to be put in hand.   (Stephen Evans)

NOTICE TO SHUNTERS.
THESE **POINTS** TO
BE LEFT SET FOR
RIGHT HAND ROAD.

Progress of the 'Prince' hauled rake of ballast wagons depicted opposite came to an abrupt halt. A faulty wheel set was diagnosed. Acquisition of sixteen modern Hudson wagons ex-RAF Alrewas in 1963 took some of the pressure off the Festiniog Railway's fleet of ancient granite wagons.

(N. Gurley)

ast continued to be purchased from British Rail, but increasing use of ballast cleaners on standard gauge brought about a steady deterioration in the quality of spent ballast vered to Minffordd. Hauling heavy loads up what has always been known as the coal road is a test for Festiniog locomotives and crews.

(N. Gurley)

Attention was being turned at this period in the mid-1960s to the spectacular two miles of track between Tan-y-Bwlch and Dduallt. S.& T. volunteers started work on the pole route and liberal doses of weedkiller were applied to the turf-covered track as a prelude to relaying work. The first half-mile was relaid by the Army as part of an exercise in September 1965.

(N. Gurley)

As relaying continued towards Dduallt, largely in the hands of volunteers with one or two staff as supervisors, varying forms of transport were used to connect with the passenger services at Tan-y-Bwlch. 'Mary Ann' was a handy personnel carrier in fine weather. Penrhyn Quarry Railway bull-head track was used throughout this section, or ex-BR softwood sleepers, most of which had become available from the Great Central li

(N. Gur

A spritely 71 years of age, ex-East Coast main line driver Bill Hoole has no problems with 'Prince' on a light morning train of three roller-bearing coaches on 23 May 1966. After seven full seasons of cative 'retirement' on the Festiniog, this was unhappily to be Bill Hoole's last year of driving, as he suffered two strokes the following Easter. He remained keenly interested in both standard and narrow gauge railways until his death in 1979.

(Tony Massau)

'Merddin Emrys' was the heavy duty performer of the mid-1960s, here photogra[...] from the observation car of a down train.

(Dr Alan Pea[...]

Wedding bells rang on 23 October 1965 for the marriage of the Festiniog Railway's General Manager, Allan Garraway, to Moyra Macmillan, and after the ceremony and reception in Portmadoc a special train took them on the first stage of their honeymoon. The groom and best man are riding on 'Prince's tender, while Moyra entertains the guests in the train!

(John Ransom

Snow covers Moelwyn Mawr (2,527') and Bach (2,334') as 'Linda' leaves Minffordd and heads across Gwyndy bank. Most of the Festiniog's dry-stone embankments have remained untouched for something like 140 years, but an occasional buttress of a different stone shows where reinforcement was considered necessary at some stage in the railway's history.

(Bob Miller)

The entry into service in 1963 of an ex-Lynton and Barnstaple Railway vehicle as a buffet car with greatly improved facilities resulted in an increasing demand for evening specials. This particular one on 24 August 1963 celebrated the working visit of the 500th 'Tadpole' - consisting of volunteers from Chace School, Enfield.

(Gil Roscoe)

On 9 June 1966 Blaenau Ffestiniog Music Society used [an] evening special to celebrate a highly successful presentation of 'The Mikado' produced by Allan Garraway. The music society and a model railway club are but two of many local activities strongly supported [by] Festiniog Railway staff over the years.
(Geoff Charles)

Members of the local Women's Institutes like to have opportunities to appear in period costume and are sometimes called upon to help the Festiniog relive its past. Here some extras are being escorted to the service train after appearing with 'Prince' in a BBC television production.
(N. Gurley)

The story of the construction of the Cob is almost as enthralling as the history of the Festiniog Railway itself, both the railway and the town of Portmadoc owing their very existence to the enterprise and determination of William Madocks. The link with Madocks became a little more tenuous in 1973 when the Welsh version Porthmadog became standard, but the railway perpetuates his name on one of the buffet cars. The others carry the equally notable Festiniog names of 'Charles Spooner' and 'Samuel Holland'.

(Bob Miller)

'Princess goes to meet her Prince' ran the headlines, and Prince Charles was probably as embarrassed about it as anybody.... Nevertheless, since the Investiture in 1969 'Princess' has earned her scrap value many times over, on display in Blaenau Ffestiniog as a constant reminder of the Festiniog Railway's existence and its unwavering determination to run trains into the town once again.   (Festiniog Railway)

The first Beyer Garratt was built in 1909 for a narrow-gauge line in Tasmania. In stc by 1930, K1 was brought back to Britain in 1947 and kept at the Gorton works of Beyer, Peacock & Co. until closure in 1966, when she was purchased by Festiniog supporters. cumbersome for present needs, she was presented on loan to the National Railway Museum York, after eleven years at Portmadoc and Boston Lodge.   (Bob Mill

ke 'Princess',
sh Pony'
cially awaits
ilding, and
refore has to
d most of her
s out of the
ic eye - but
l exposed to the
ents - in a
her of Boston
e yard. She last
d under her own
am in 1938 ; but
sh ponies are a
ent breed.
                (P.J. Lynch)

'Earl of Merioneth' was back in service in time for the extension to Dduallt on 6 April 1968, by which time 'Merddin Emrys' was in shops receiving a new boiler. This photograph in 1970 shows 'Earl' at Penrhyn crossing. Although automatic barriers were acquired for Penrhyn in the 1960s, various problems have delayed their installation.

(Stephen Evans)

Arriving on
Festiniog metals in
October 1967, Alco
2-6-2- Tank
'Mountaineer' proved
a useful acquisition,
but the exceptionally
large diameter boiler
tubes made her even
more prone to start
lineside fires than
the other
locomotives. Efforts
to control this led,
in 1971, to the
provision of a spark
arrester; thereafter
in extreme conditions
forestry patrols were
only able to report
extinguishing dozens
of fires - instead of
hundreds....
            (N. Gurley)

By the summer of 1973 all active steam locomotives had been converted to burn oil - not always as obviously as 'Blanche' in this photograph. The average rate of consumption was just over four gallons per mile for 'Merddin Emrys' just under four for 'Mountaineer' and new 'Earl of Merioneth' (1979), and approximately two for 'Linda' and 'Blanche'. (N. Gurley)

ersion to oil firing was an obvious answer to the forestry fire problem, and n Lodge staff set about the conversion of 'Linda' with varying degrees of siasm. The results exceeded most expectations, and the advantages in terms ficiency and cleanliness were greatly appreciated by most loco crews. A few en departed in search of coal burners elsewhere, but others soon took their . (Geoff Charles)

On passenger work, diesel 'Upnor Castle' uses only a gallon of the same oil, but without the addition of waste, to cover at least four miles - a startling indication of the relative inefficiency of the steam locomotive even after allowing for weight of train and other factors. This Planet is normally only used on reduced-fare services or when a steam locomotive has to be replaced or assisted.

(N. Gurley)

The transshipment sidings at Minffordd have inevitably changed their character with the change in fuel, providing storage capacity for well over 40,000 gallons. Processed waste oil purchased commercially and 'clean' waste brought by Festiniog supporters is added to the gas oil and helps to keep the running costs at an acceptable level. A network of collection points throughout Britain is being developed by the railway's Waste Oil Co-ordinator and the Road Transport Dept. (N. Gurley)

The interchange station at Minffordd realy comes to life when British Rail bring
excursions up the Cambrian Coast line for a trip on the Festiniog. This one on
3 October 1970 was an extension of a Talyllyn Railway Preservation Society A.G.M.
special.
                                                                    (N. Gurley)

68

Tan-y-Bwlch, too, has its extremely busy moments, such as this occasion on 12 June 1977 when the Main Line Steam Trust brought 997 passengers and used fleets of buses between Blaenau Ffestiniog and Tan-y-Bwlch. Now that the Festiniog is a two-ended railway, with road access at Tanygrisiau as well as Porthmadog, such excursionists are only likely to see Tan-y-Bwlch from the carriage windows.

(N. Gurley)

For reasons probably forgotten by all concerned, 'Moelwyn' assists 'Blanche' into Tan-y-Bwlch, while a down train stands ready to leave for Porthmadog. The Ffestiniog is often stated to be a right hand running railway. Not so; each passing place has its most convenient operating line designated the Through road, and the other the loop. Passenger trains not crossing, or due to cross a non-passenger train, take the Through road. When two passenger trains are crossing the up train normally takes the Through road. Thus right hand running is observed at Minffordd and Tan-y-Bwlch, left hand running at Penrhyn (latterly, but due for closure), Rhiw Goch and Dduallt. There is talk of altering Tan-y-Bwlch in the early 1980s.

(N. Gurley)

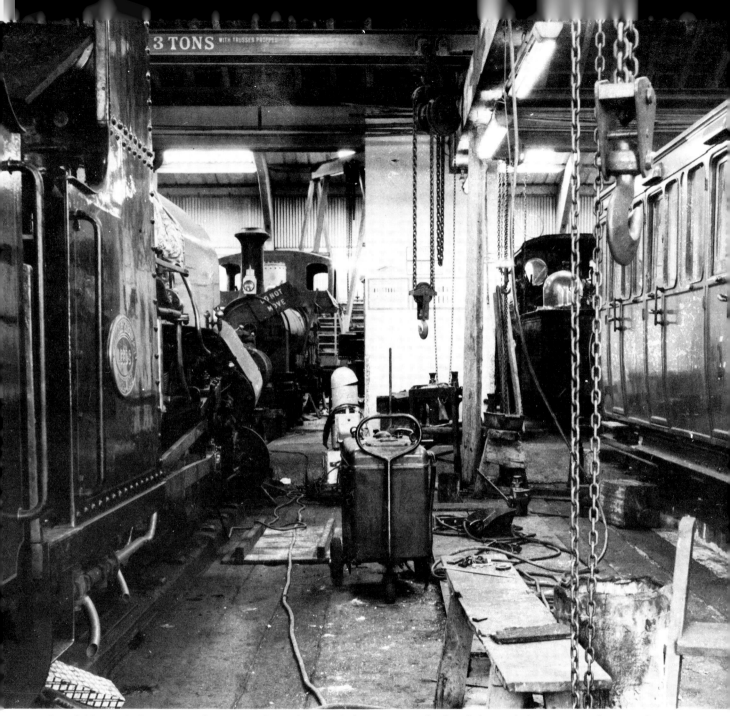

Lunchtime at Boston Lodge erecting shop, with a great deal of inactivity centred around 'Blanche', new 'Earl of Merioneth', 'Linda' and one of the bow-sider coaches of 1875. More than half of the Festiniog Railway's permanent staff, totalling 57 in 1979, are based at Boston Lodge.

(E.N. Kneale)

Volunteer fireman Sue adroitly exchanges tokens
with the Minffordd signalman at (a very nominal)
10 miles per hour. On the present-day Festiniog,
any sufficiently competent and dedicated
volunteer can progress through the grades to
driver.   (N. Gurley)

With the late afternoon sun highlighting a
motley assortment of coaches, 'Merddin Emrys'
leaves the through road at Minffordd bound for
Porthmadog.   (N. Gurley)

Since the start of 1965, volunteers of the railway's Civil Engineering Group, (known from the beginning as the Deviationists), with a gradually increasing amount of professional assistance, have been constructing the new line between Dduallt and Tanygrisiau, deviating round the valley flooded by the C.E.G.B. 'Pumped storage' hydro-electric scheme. The spiral at Dduallt was constructed entirely by 'pick and shovel' methods, with some help from a qualified but unpaid shot firer, and remains as permanent a monument to their efforts as the Cob is to Madocks's.

(N. Gurley)

While the new line was under construction, trains terminated at Dduallt; a more unlikely place for a terminus is hard to imagine. With no road access and, initially, no services such as water or electricity, the serving hatches in the buffet cars had an important function to perform.

(E.N. Kneale)

With the spiral completed, thought turned to the boring of the new Moelwyn tunnel, and an offer by three Cornish mining experts to do the job was gratefully accepted. An ex-N.C.B. mines diesel, later to be named 'Moel Hebog', here propels a rake of tunnelling equipment towards the construction complex, past a work site still known a Two Trees. The second of these has now disappeared as unfortunately it grew where the centre-line of the track had to be laid.

(Festiniog Railway)

The Wales Tourist Board made some useful grants towards the new line works and naturally expected to see trains operating as soon as possible. In the summer of 1975 a shuttle service was operated between Dduallt and Gelliwiog which was the closest convenient point to the tunnel site - using 'Moel Hebog' and a newly-constructed coach fitted for push-pull working. Most passengers showed a marked reluctance to change trains at Dduallt for the sake of an extra mile of track - even round Britain's only railway spiral - and the service ended in 1976. Tunnel rock was being tipped at the top end of Dduallt station and the shuttle service would have complicated the operation of the rock trains.

(Festiniog Railway)

Tunnel South site took on a markedly industrial appearance as the tunnel boring proceeded. The rock from the tunnel (train on right) was tipped into a hopper for screening into three grades, and the middle grade was handed over to the permanent way gang in trainloads of ballast. The boring of an eight foot square pilot tunnel took eight months; enlarging to full size and shotcreting vital areas took a further twelve years.

Below : on one of its rare outdoor appearances, the compressed air-powered mine loader, used for clearing blasted rock from the working face, proves itself quite capable of shunting four wagons loaded with ballast.   (N. Gurley)

ng before the
nnel was finished,
e formation on to a
te known as Buarth
lyn had been
mpleted and track
id. A temporary
atform and run-
und loop enabled
ssenger trains to
n to Llyn Ystradau
soon as the tunnel
s opened in the
mmer of 1977.
(Festiniog Railway)

re was still
nty of scope for
unteers on the new
e. A Crusaders'
k camp constructed
of the major
verts near
ygrisiau during
ust 1976 and,
ether with
ilar groups, have
vided an invaluable
mer work-force
r many years.
(Festiniog Railway)

Two small Simplex diesels were acquired by Col. Andrew Campbell of Dduallt Manor in 1966 and one was later given to the railway for Deviation work. Named 'Jane', it is here helping to receive gravel at Minffordd for new line culvert construction.

(Bob Miller)

Having made up the train, 'Jane' hands over to 'Mountaineer for the main line journey to Dduallt; the train also includes culvert pipes. There are at least two dozen culverts under the new line, although three of them are actually to permit sheep, rather than water, to pass from one side of the line to the other.

(Bob Miller

The first steam locomotive through the tunnel was 'Mountaineer' on 28 May 1977. Also in this scene are the profile gauge with feelers fully extended, the BEV battery electric loco used by the miners throughout the boring, and 'Moelwyn'.
(Festiniog Railway)

The section of r
line behind the
power station wa
subject to sever
restrictions
concerning blast
and other aspect
construction. T
work was done by
labour force of
40 men employed
the Jobs Creatio
Programme, manag
under contract b
McAlpines. Behi
the power statio
the work entaile
building subterr
bridges over the
pipes feeding th
power station fr
the upper reserv
(N. Gu

The grand opening of Tanygrisiau station took place in heavy rain on 24 June 1978, 24 years to the day after Alan Pegler had taken over control of the Festiniog Railway Company, and it was appropriate that he was amongst the distinguished gathering of Festiniog personalities present. 200 'Deviationists' held their own celebration in the centre of Dduallt spiral the same evening. (Festiniog Railway)

he time the blizzards of early 1979 arrived, the outstanding work on the new
took the form of landscaping, improvements to culvert head walls and
rance of untidy work sites.　　　　　　　　　　　　　　　　　　(N. Gurley)

With the help of Crosville Motor Services, Tanygrisiau station has become the focal point of Blaenau Ffestiniog's tourist attractions. Visits to the nearby power station can be arranged, and buses leave regularly for the Stwlan Dam, Llechwedd Slate Caverns and Gladdfa Ganol (Mountain Tourist Centre with narrow-gauge locomotive collection) as well as the British Rail station. Little wonder that on a fine day in August the late afternoon trains back to Porthmadog take on a 'rush-hour' appearance.   (N. Gurley)

'Blanche' passing Campbell's Platform and heading for Dduallt with the first train of the day. Except at a few locations such as Dduallt spiral and the inaccessible curves below Tan-y-Bwlch, the sun only shines on the smokebox d of up trains early in the morning.   (N. Gu

The most modern of the Festiniog Railway diesels, answering to but not actually displaying the name 'Sandra', photographed above Garnedd tunnel, near Tan-y-Bwlch, with a train used for pointing the brick portal arches in April 1979. (N. Gurley)

At best the section of track between Tanygrisiau and Blaenau Ffestiniog can be said to enhance the contrasting nature of the Festiniog Railway's scenery. Some basic relaying was put in hand during the summer of 1975, this particular party of volunteers being the annual work camp from Brambleton Model Railway Club, Harpenden, August regulars since 1962. (Roger Smith)

Soon after leaving Rhiw Goch passing loop with an up train, 'Linda' heads through the forestry plantations around Cei Mawr. Down trains give two long whistles here to alert the signalman. The track is to the Festiniog's highest standard, with new 60 lb/yard flat-bottom rail fastened to new Jarrah sleepers on a good bed of clean granite ballast. Unfortunately, new rail has risen to prices beyond the Railway's reach and second-hand 75lb flat-bottom has become the standard for the 1980s.

(N. Gurley)

'Merddin Emrys' coasts down among the old oaks of Coed Dduallt, on the upper part of
Dduallt spiral. Outside of station limits there is only one curve on the Festiniog
Railway's main line tighter than Dingle. When trains are crossing at Dduallt the Up
usually arrives first, and passengers find it an interesting experience to sit and follow
the progress of the Down train as it trundles round the almost continuous curves of the
spiral.

(N. Gurley)

89

No Festiniog pictorial album would be complete without a photograph of 'Britomart', purchased by a consortium of staff and volunteers from Pen-y-Orsedd slate quarry in 1965. Typical of the many small Hunslets once used in the North Wales quarries, she was overhauled and turned out in a smart blue livery for steaming on special occasions.

(N. Gurley)

ightest curve on the line is Tyler's, situated between Plas Tan-y-Bwlch and
alt opened in 1963 to serve the Plas. Tyler's was named after the Board of
's inspecting officer who authorised the Festiniog to carry passengers in
'Mountaineer' is the locomotive, seen here in early June 1978. (N. Gurley)

After extensive trials, tests and ceremonies, the new 'Earl of Merioneth' entered passenger service on 19 July 1979, exactly one hundred years after Boston Lodge had completed its previous new steam locomotive.
(N. Gurley)

As centenarian 'Merddin Emrys' passes Boston Lodge original engine shed (now used for winter carriage storage but eventually due to be restored to motive power duties), it can be seen that Festiniog clearances are indeed limited. Many of the cuttings were designed and constructed for slate wagons less than 3' wide (later types were 4' wide) and even in 1865 the passenger trains fitted them hand in glove.

(N. Gurley)

The Festiniog Railway Society celebrated its 25 years of active support for the Railway over the week-end of 15-16 September 1979. Many of the special attractions were at Boston Lodge and the first batch of visitors arrived in the same two coaches as operated the first trains across the Cob in July 1955. With roof, diesel engine, vacuum brake and nameplates (and ear protectors for the driver) the Simplex presented a very different appearance, but it was none the less a nostalgic occasion. (N. Gurley)